Christmas Programs
for
Sacrament Meetings
(Resource Manual only!)

Compiled by C. Michael Perry

Contributing Authors
Charlee Cardon Wilson,
Myrth Burr
and
Carolyn Gifford

ZION Book Works
An Imprint of Leicester Bay Books

Salt Lake City

Christmas Programs for Sacrament Meetings
© 1995 by C. Michael Perry

CAUTION: Professionals and amateurs are hereby warned that

Christmas Programs
for Sacrament Meetings

Table Of Contents

THE INNKEEPER'S STORY by Charlee Wilson

CHARACTERS: NARRATOR, INNKEEPER + CHOIR (SATB)

NOTE: This was meant to provide a framework for a Christmas Sacrament meeting or Fireside, and the music should be selected to fit the available talents and tastes of those performing it.

Duplication of TWO copies included in Production Package: $3.00. Order # 4041.

THE INNKEEPER'S CHILDREN by Charlee Wilson

CHARACTERS: NARRATOR, SARAH (younger child), AARON (older child), SHEPHERD BOY (with Lamb), INNKEEPER (non-speaking pantomime), JOSEPH (non-speaking pantomime), MARY (non-speaking pantomime), SHEPHERDS (non-speaking pantomime, optional) + CHOIR (SATB)

NOTE: This is a variation on the INNKEEPER program, planned for a children's production, using music of your choice by a children's choir or adult choir. This is more suitable for a stage set than a chapel setting.

Duplication of NINE copies included in Production Package: $8.00 Order # 4042.

SEEK HIM WITH HASTE by Carolyn Gifford

CHARACTERS: Reader 1 (Female), Reader 2 (Male), Reader 3 (Female or Male), + Choir (SATB) and soloists (optional)

NOTE: This is a format or structure for the addition of appropriate Christmas songs, carols or hymns. You may use the songs suggested in the script or substitute some of your own choosing. Has original songs. ($3.00 each copy, each song)

Duplication of FOUR copies included in Production
Package: $4.00 Order # 4043.

THAT IT MIGHT BE FULFILLED... by Myrth Burr

CHARACTERS: Reader, Narrator, Children in Primary
(maybe only selected classes), + CHOIR (SATB)

NOTE: This is a format or structure for the addition of
appropriate Christmas songs, carols or hymns. You may
use the songs suggested in the script or substitute some of
your own choosing.

Duplication of THREE copies included in Production
Package: $3.00 Order # 4044.

THERE WILL BE PEACE by Myrth Burr

CHARACTERS: READER 1, READER 2, CHOIR (SATB)

NOTE: This is a format or structure for the addition of
appropriate Christmas songs, carols or hymns. You may
use the songs suggested in the script or substitute some of
your own choosing.

Duplication of THREE copies included in Production
Package: $3.00 Order # 4045.

AMERICA'S FIRST CHRISTMAS by Myrth Burr

CHARACTERS: NARRATOR, READER (is the voice of
Samuel The Lamanite, the people of Nephi III, Jesus
Christ), + CHOIR (SATB) with optional soloists

NOTE: This was meant to provide a framework for a
Christmas Sacrament meeting or Fireside, and the music
should be selected to fit the available talents and tastes of
those performing it.

Duplication of THREE copies included in Production
Package: $3.00 Order # 4046.

LIFT UP YOUR HEAD
AND BE OF GOOD CHEER by Carolyn Gifford

> CHARACTERS: Five READERS + CHOIR (SATB), SOLOIST, ORGANIST

> NOTE: This program was designed originally to involve the Bishop's family. His wife and each of his children took turns narrating the words. It is easily adaptable to any family but we still recommend that the long section in the middle of the piece be spoken by the Bishop of the Ward. Has original songs. See Production Package for prices and details.

> Duplication of FIVE copies included in Production Package: $5.00 Order # 4047.

The manuscript copies you will order from this manual are 8 1/2 X 11 in size, unbound in a PDF file that will be emailed to you upon payment of the Production Package fee..

HOW TO ORDER

1.   Telephone orders may be placed by calling 801-282-8159. We will send the material to you by email. We will then send you a PayPal invoice.

2.   If you wish to mail us your order, write out the quantity, titles, order numbers and prices of the readings you want. Enclose a payment by CHECK with your order, or ask to receive a PayPal invoice.

3.   There are no shipping charges, but Utah Sales Tax will be added to every order.

4.   REMEMBER: you may not, in any way, copy or reproduce the readings/skits or music in or from this manual. Nor may you copy or reproduce any of the material you order from this manual without paying the small Production Package fee. If you do so you will be breaking the law and are subject to fines and fees! If you happen to lose a copy or damage a copy, or simply need an extra, please contact us and purchase the copy needed. Be safe! Don't break the law! Copying books in whole or in part robs the author of his livelihood and is illegal and immoral.

5. Please, also remember that the songs used in the readings, in many cases, are copyrighted. Purchase copies from the publishers or their music store representatives.

THE INNKEEPER'S STORY
by Charlee Wilson

CHARACTERS
NARRATOR
INNKEEPER
CHOIR

NOTE: This presentation is suitable for Sacrament Meeting Services, using choir and narration. Choir numbers, congregational hymns, and instrumental music is suggested, however, other musical selections may be substituted as desired. This was meant to provide a framework for a Christmas Sacrament meeting or Fireside, and the music should be selected to fit the available talents and tastes of those performing it.

*(Traditional arrangement of **O Come O Come Emmanuel** under narration)*

NARRATOR: Remember, O Lord, what is come upon us: consider, and behold our reproach. Our inheritance is turned to strangers, our houses to aliens.We are orphans and fatherless, our mothers are as widows. Our fathers have sinned,...and we have borne their iniquities. The joy of our heart is ceased; our dance is turned into mourning. The crown is fallen from our head: woe unto us, that we have sinned! For this our heart is faint; for these things our eyes are dim. Thou, O Lord, remainest forever; thy throne from generation to generation. Wherefore dost

1

thou forget us for ever, and forsake us so long time? Turn thou us unto thee, O Lord, and we shall be turned; renew our days of old. But thou hast utterly rejected us; thou art very wroth against us. (Lamentations 5)

> *(Music to the introduction of the Natalie Sleeth arrangement of **O Come O Come Emmanuel** under narration)*

O Lord, how long shall I cry, and thou wilt not hear! even cry out unto thee of violence, and thou wilt not save!

O COME O COME EMMANUEL (Choir)

INNKEEPER: Times were troubled in Judea. There was poverty and disease. Deep despair had settled like a cloud over the country. Old men..my father..talked of a Redeemer, one who would come and save Judah from its oppressed state...no, not just Judah, the WORLD! Ha! Fairy tales. Fantasies! I had been raised on them. "Trust in God," Father said, "Study the words of the prophets. Watch and pray - your faith will be rewarded." Children's stories! One could not feed a family on faith. Oh, I paid my tithes to please my father. Now and then, I even attended the synagogue, but those times were rare. So, while the foolish old men studied their books, discussed the ancient prophecies, and waited for this Champion to appear and save us all, I worked! I was no dreamer, I had learned early in life that a man must earn his way with his own sweat. I slaved. My wife slaved. Even my children were not spared toil. My inn was the finest in Bethlehem.

The Innkeepers Story

I was not a rich man....who could be rich in such a society...but I had learned. Render unto Caesar that which is Caesar's. Render unto Herod that which is Herod's. Render unto God that which is God's. The residue, if any, was mine. With it, we were permitted to live in relative peace. I could put food on the table, clothes on our backs, bribe a few minor officials, and even save a coin or two on occasion. I was content.

*(Intro to **Little Town of Bethlehem** under narrator.)*
NARRATOR: And it came to pass in those days that there went out a decree from Caesar Augustus, that all the world should be taxed.And all went to be taxed, every one into his own city. And Joseph also went up from Galilee, out of the city of Nazareth, into Judea, unto the city of David, which is called Bethlehem...To be taxed with Mary his espoused wife, being great with child.

OH LITTLE TOWN OF BETHLEHEM (Choir)

INNKEEPER: The taxes! Oh, what a wonderful thing for innkeepers! People poured into the city. I raised my prices. I only accepted the wealthiest travelers - all others, were turned away. My rooms were filled. Even the benches in the dining hall were rented. My family moved into my father's room so that I could rent our own sleeping quarters...and still the travelers came...a parade of weary, travel-stained strangers plodding endlessly through the streets. At first, when they would knock, I would greet them at the door, but as the days wore on, I simply began crying out from wherever I was working...No Room! Then, one night, as we were serving dinner, another traveler came knocking. The noise inside was so great that my shout of "no room" could not be heard. I decided to ignore him. Soon, I reasoned, he would tire and leave. But another knock came, and then another. It was with considerable irritation that I finally left my duties as host and went to turn the traveler away. To this day, I cannot explain what came over me when I opened the door. My angry cry froze in my throat. On my doorstep stood a man leading a donkey. On the back of the small beast was his wife. It was apparent that she was with child and that her time was very near. Fatigue showed in their faces. They were hungry and dusty....no different from dozens of others I had turned away that day...and yet...I found myself searching my mind for a place they might lodge. There was truly not a corner to be had in the inn. I was just about to turn them away, when I remembered the stable. There was fresh straw, and a roof out of the wind. I directed the weary couple to the stable and went back to my duties.

*(Intro to **Silent Night** under narration)*

NARRATOR: And so it was that while they were there, the days were accomplished that she should be delivered. And she brought forth her firstborn son, and wrapped him in swaddling clothes, and laid him in the manger; because there was no room for them in the inn.

The Innkeepers Story

SILENT NIGHT (Choir, Congregation, soloist)

*(**O Holy Night** under narration)*

NARRATOR: And there were in the same country shepherds abiding in the fields, keeping watch over their flock by night. And, lo, the angel of the Lord came upon them, and the glory of the Lord shone round about them: and they were sore afraid. And the angel said unto them, Fear not: for, behold, I bring you good tidings of great joy, which shall be to all people. For unto you is born this day in the city of David, a Saviour, which is Christ the Lord. And this shall be a sign unto you; Ye shall find the babe wrapped in swaddling clothes, lying in a manger. And suddenly there was with the angel a multitude of the heavenly host praising God, and saying, Glory to God in the highest, and on earth peace, good will toward men.

WHILE BY MY SHEEP (Choir)
or
ANGELS WE HAVE HEARD ON HIGH (Congregation)

*(Intro to **Away in A Manger** under narration.)*

NARRATOR: And it came to pass, as the angels were gone away from them into heaven, the shepherds said one to another, Let us now go even unto Bethlehem, and see this thing which is come to pass, which the Lord hath made known unto us. And they came with haste, and found Mary, and Joseph, and the babe lying in the manger.

Christmas Programs For Sacrament Meetings

AWAY IN A MANGER (Congregation)

INNKEEPER: It was late. The inn had been busy all day. I was tired. I stepped out into the cool night air. The courtyard was bright with moonlight. I looked up and saw not the moon, but a star more brilliant than any I had ever seen lighting the night sky. The light it shed lit up the countryside. I heard footsteps on the road beside the inn. How strange, I thought, who would be traveling at so late an hour? I opened the gate and looked down the road. Indeed, strange! There were shepherds passing by the inn. They were silent, except for the shuffle of their feet as they passed. Even the lambs some of them carried didn't make a sound. Where were they going at so late? Why had they left their flocks? Finally, I stopped a young shepherd boy and inquired of him. He told a fantastic story of angel choirs appearing in the heavens, of a babe, a King, born in a stable. The boy hurried on. He was going to worship the new King. I stood in the road speechless. Had the shepherds gone mad? A King born in a stable? Where would his kingdom be? Over whom would he rule? Could this be the great King and Redeemer of whom the old men spoke?

ONLY A BABY CAME (Duet or Small group)

INNKEEPER: I had to see this thing for myself. I hurried after the shepherds. There in my own stable, I found the couple to whom I had given shelter. On the straw, in the manger, a baby lay. Not a word was spoken as shepherds knelt around the babe. There was a sweet peace about the scene. I stared in wonder.

BABY WHAT YOU GONNA BE? (Choir)

(We Three Kings under narration)
NARRATOR: Now when Jesus was born in Bethlehem of Judea in the days of Herod the king, behold, there came wise men from the east to Jerusalem. Saying, Where is he that is born King of the Jews? for we have seen his star in the east, and are come to worship him. And when they were come into the house, they saw the young child with Mary his mother, and fell down, and worshipped him: and when they had opened their treasures, they presented unto him gifts; gold, and frankincense, and myrrh.

DESERT NOEL (Choir)
or
WITH WONDERING AWE (Congregation)
or
WE THREE KINGS (Mens group)

INNKEEPER: I continued to watch in silence as people from the humblest shepherd to great kings from the East came to pay homage to this little child. Suddenly, I heard my father's voice speaking the words of Isaiah.. The very words that I had ridiculed as being foolish fancies for old men and children.

*(**Joy to the World** under narration)*

The people that walked in darkness have seen a great light: they that dwell in the land of the shadow of death, upon them hath the light shined. For unto us a child is born, unto us a son is given: and the government shall be upon his shoulder: and his name shall be called Wonderful, Counsellor, The mighty God, The everlasting Father, The Prince of Peace. Of the increase of his government and peace there shall be no end.

FOR UNTO US A CHILD IS BORN (Choir)

INNKEEPER: I was as one who had walked in darkness. I was like a sleeper who had finally awakened to a glorious new dawn. My heart melted within my breast. I too fell to my knees to worship the Son of God. When I rose, I was a changed man. Love for my Father in Heaven filled my entire being. I too wanted to bring something to this babe. But, of all the earthly treasures I had accumulated, none were worthy gifts. They had to bring something to the Son of God, but I acquired with greed and avarice at the expense of my fellow man.

JESUS GIFT (Choir with soloist)

*(**Come Follow Me** under narration)*

NARRATOR: Turn ye even to me with all your heart...Cast away from you all your transgressions, whereby ye have transgressed; and make you a new heart and a new spirit: for why will ye die, O house of Israel? For I have no pleasure in the death of him that dieth, saith the Lord God: wherefore turn your-selves, and live ye. Again, words of the prophets, taught me by my father provided my answer...I turned from my transgressions. I began teaching my own children the things my father had taught me. I dedicated my life to service of my fellow man. Guests at the inn these days are usually of a humbler sort than before. We, of necessity set a simpler table. Nevertheless, what we have, we share with the strangers who come to our door. Before, I was content with my life, but today, I am truly happy. Today, I share with all who will listen the story of a baby born in my stable, right here in Bethlehem.

COME FOLLOW ME (Choir)

The End

THE INNKEEPER'S CHILDREN
by Charlee Wilson

CHARACTERS

NARRATOR

SARAH (younger child)

AARON (older child)

SHEPHERD BOY (with Lamb)

INNKEEPER (non-speaking pantomime)

JOSEPH (non-speaking pantomime)

MARY (non-speaking pantomime)

SHEPHERDS (non-speaking pantomime, optional)

[This is a variation on the INNKEEPER program, planned for a children's production, using music of your choice by a children's choir or adult choir. This is more suitable for a stage set than a chapel setting. NINE copies required]

NARRATOR: Remember, O Lord, what is come upon us: consider, and behold our reproach. Our inheritance is turned to strangers, our houses to aliens. We are orphans and fatherless, our mothers are as widows. Our fathers have sinned,...and we have borne their iniquities. The joy of our heart is ceased; our dance is turned into mourning. The crown is fallen from our head: woe unto us, that we have sinned! For this our heart is faint; for these things our eyes are dim. Thou, O Lord, remainest forever; thy throne from generation to generation. Wherefore dost thou forget us for ever, and forsake us so long time? Turn thou us unto thee, O Lord, and we shall be turned; renew our days of old. aBut thou hast utterly rejected us; thou art very wroth against us. (Lamentations 5)

(Old version of O **Come O Come Emmanuel** under narration.)

O Lord, how long shall I cry, and thou wilt not hear! even cry out unto thee of violence, and thou wilt not save!

O COME O COME EMMANUEL (Choir)(Natalie Sleeth Arrangement)

AARON: It's a hard time in Judea. People are poor, some are sick. Grandfather says they are poor in spirit and sick at heart because of how things are for Israel right now. *(to Sarah)* Grandfather says that we need the Redeemer to come.
SARAH: What's the Redeemer, Aaron?
AARON: Grandfather says the Redeemer is the Messiah who will come to save Judah, well, not just Judah, the whole world.
SARAH: Save them from what? *(looks around fearfully)* Is something chasing them?
AARON: No, silly, the Messiah will save us all from oppression.
SARAH: What's o-op-*(stumbles over the word)*, what's that?
AARON: I'm not sure, I think it means that people boss you around all the time and make you carry heavy stuff,

11

and don't let you play what you want.

SARAH: You mean like Father making us to do chores? *(with anticipation)* Will the Redeemer save us from chores?

AARON: Of course not! Everyone has to do chores. It's just that, it's not right when some people tell other people how to live and pray and...Oh, you'll understand when you're older.

SARAH: You always say that? I'll bet you don't understand either. Besides, I like the way we live. Father says we have the finest inn in Bethlehem. Mother just made me a new dress and I might get to have a kitten for my birthday. I don't think I want to be saved from that.

AARON: You sound just like Father. He says that the Redeemer is just a story for old men and children - a Fairy tale. He thinks Grandfather is foolish to spend so much time studying the words of the prophets.

SARAH: Father goes to the temple sometimes too.

AARON: Yes, I know, and he pays his tithes, but he only does it to keep Grandfather from preaching to him. Father believes that everyone must earn their own way - not wait for some Champion to come along and do all the work for them.

SARAH: Boy, do we work! I wouldn't mind if somebody came along and did my work.

AARON: Why do you think our inn is the best one in town? We work hard to make it the best. Father says that no one can get rich in our society, but *(strikes an adult pose and mimics a parent lecturing)* we have good food, nice clothes, and a roof over our heads and we are better off than most of our neighbors, so we shouldn't complain.

NARRATOR: And it came to pass in those days that there went out a decree from Caesar Augustus, that all the world should be taxed. And all went to be taxed, every one into his own city. And Joseph also went up from Galilee, out of the city of Nazareth, into Judea, unto the city of David, which is called Bethlehem....to be taxed with his espoused wife, being great with child.

AARON: The taxes! What a wonderful thing for innkeepers.

SARAH: Well, it's not so wonderful for innkeepers' daughters. All I ever do is chores and more chores!

AARON: You don't have it so hard. Try trading places with me! Clean the stable! Haul the water! Bring the firewood! I've never seen so many people in the city before.

SARAH: Well, I wish they would all go home. I want my own room back. It's not fair that Father rented my room to that horrible man and his fat wife.

AARON: Oh, quit complaining! How do you think Father got the money for that new dress you've been bragging about? He says we've got to make the most of this opportunity. He's only accepting the richest guests. He's raised his prices, and says we can stack people like cordwood and they'll still be willing to pay.

SARAH: *(gloomy)* I know, this morning, he rented the benches in the dining hall. If anyone else comes he'll probably move me out in the streets so he can rent my pallet in the kitchen.

AARON: *(mischievously)* Well, there's always the stable.

SARAH: Oh no! He wouldn't. He couldn't put me in that dirty place!

AARON: Dirty! Not after I spent all day cleaning it. I even took a nap down there on the new straw. It's not so bad. It's certainly quieter than Grandfather's room. He snores!

SARAH: I don't care. I won't go! I'll run away...I'll....

AARON: Oh be quiet! I was just teasing, besides, Father isn't accepting any more guests. Every time someone knocks, he shouts "No Room!" I think that even he realizes we're as full as we can get.

SARAH: Don't be so sure. He's talking to a traveler right now....See

> *(She points lights up on Innkeeper and Joseph mime talk or frozen. This may also be done as a silhouette show, with the adults only visible as shadows on a screen.)*

AARON: He looks so tired. I wonder how far he's walked today.

SARAH: Look, there's a lady with him...on the donkey. Poor donkey. I'll bet he's hungry, and the lady is so pretty. I wish they could have my room instead of those other people.

AARON: Don't be silly. Even if it was empty, they don't look like they have the rent Father is charging.

SARAH: Look! Father is turning them away. Where will they go? All the inns are full. Are they going to have to sleep in the street?

AARON: No, maybe not. There's the stable, remember!

The Innkeepers Children

Father, wait!

(As the next passage is read, lights on SARAH and AARON dim, the stable is brought onto the stage, Mary and Joseph take their places at the manger and the Star is raised behind the scene. This may be done on one side of the stage under soft lights or in silhouette. Appropriate music may be played in the background or hummed by a choir.)

NARRATOR: And so it was that while they were there, the days were accomplished that she should be delivered. And she brought forth her firstborn son, and wrapped him in swaddling clothes, and laid him in the manger; because there was no room for them in the inn.

(A shepherd scene may be staged on the opposite side of the stage from the manger scene. It may also be done in silhouette.)

And there were in the same country shepherds abiding in the fields, keeping watch over their flocks by night. And, lo, the angel of the Lord came upon them, and the glory of the Lord shone round about them: and they were sore afraid. And the angel said unto them, Fear not: for, behold, I bring you good tidings of great joy, which shall be to all people. For unto you is born this day in the city of David, a Saviour, which is Christ the Lord. And this shall be a sign unto you: Ye shall find the babe wrapped in swaddling clothes, lying in a manger. And suddenly there was with the angel a multitude of the heavenly host praising God and saying, Glory to God in the highest, and on earth peace, good will toward men.

(If desired, a choir selection, such as **Angels We Have Heard On High**, may be performed here.)

And it came to pass, as the angels were gone away from them into heaven, the shepherds said one to another, let us now go even unto Bethlehem, and see this thing which is come to pass, which the Lord hath made known unto us. And they came with haste, and found Mary, and Joseph, and the babe lying in the manger.

SARAH: *(Lights up on SARAH and AARON)* Aaron, come quick. Look - out on the road. There are people.

AARON: Shh! What are you doing up so late? What people?

SARAH: I couldn't sleep. I heard something. Anyway, you're up too.

AARON: Yeah, I woke up and it was light outside. I thought it was morning. I've never seen the moon so bright.

SARAH: But it's not the moon. Look! It's a great big star...and there are lots of people on the road. See!

AARON: That's funny. It's so late.

SARAH: They'll never find a room now.

AARON: They don't look like regular travelers...they look like...shepherds! What are they doing in town? It's lambing season. They should be up in the hills with their flocks. Look! There's Father talking to one of them.

> *(Father and adult shepherd are lighted or silhouetted in the background)*

The Innkeepers Children

SARAH: Oh no! I knew it, he's going to rent my pallet, and now the stable is full too. Where will I sleep?

AARON: Come on, let's find out what's happening.

(Shepherd boy enters, carrying a lamb).

AARON: *(to shepherd boy)* Hello. What's going on? How come you're out so late? Are you lost?

SARAH: I hope you have a place to stay. This inn is full...and it's very very expensive.

BOY: Oh, we're not staying in town.

SARAH: Oh good!...I mean...Can I pet your lamb?

BOY: Sure. He's a birthday present.

SARAH: Boy! You're so lucky...all I get is a kitten.

BOY: No, he's not my birthday present. He's a birthday present for the new king.

AARON: What new king?

BOY: The new king that's been born in Bethlehem. My father is taking me to see him....Say, didn't you hear the angels?

AARON: A King born here? Angels? What are you talking about?

BOY: Listen. We were all out in the hills. I was sleeping. My father was watching the sheep. Suddenly, This bright light shines in my eyes and wakes me up

SARAH: (points) It's the star.

BOY: No, it wasn't. It was much brighter. It lit up the whole sky. It hurt my eyes to look up at it, but I squinted real hard... and looked... and... there was an angel!

AARON: *(skeptically)* A real angel? Where was your father?

BOY: He was right there. He saw it too. There were lots of angels. All the shepherds saw them. Really! Ask my Father!

AARON: *(still not sure what to believe)* So, what happened then? Did you talk to him - the angel, I mean.

BOY: Well, naturally, we were all sore afraid....

SARAH: You were what?

BOY: Sore afraid...well, that's what my father said we were...actually, I was just scared. But the angel told us to Fear not. He said he was bringing good tidings of great joy for all people.

SARAH: He was bringing what?

BOY: Good tidings. That's angel talk. He means he had good news for everyone. I figured since he said it was for all people, he would have stopped at your place too.

AARON: *(scans the sky)* Well, maybe, he's running late. What kind of good tidings did he bring?

BOY: He said that there was a new king born in Bethlehem, a Savior who is Christ the Lord. He said that the king was lying in a stable in a manger bed.

AARON: A king? In a manger? What kind of king sleeps in a manger? Are you sure you got the message right?

BOY: Honest, that's what he said. My father says it must be the Good Shepherd that Grandfather talked about. He's a shepherd and a king. That's probably why the angels came and told us shepherds first. *(looks to the Innkeeper and Shepherd in the background)*...Oh, my father is leaving, I'd better go take my present to the new king.

AARON: You're really going to give a lamb to a king?

The Innkeepers Children

BOY: Sure, if He's the Good Shepherd, He'll know how to take care of it....Bye.

> *(exits)*

SARAH: Come on, Aaron, let's go see the new king!

> *(Children cross to manger scene where shepherds are kneeling and standing.)*

AARON: Wait, Sarah! We can't go over there. Look, everyone has brought gifts. We don't have anything to give the King.

SARAH: But look, Aaron, there's father! *(Points to the innkeeper kneeling at the manger). (hushed)* He's crying!

> *(Innkeeper looks at children, motions them to come near. The children go to their father, look reverently into the manger as music comes up. Choir may hum or sing quietly as scene freezes for a moment)*

(Come Follow Me under narration)

NARRATOR: Turn ye even to me with all your heart...Cast away from you all your transgressions, whereby ye have transgressed; and make you a new heart and a new spirit: for why will ye die, O house of Israel? For I have no pleasure in the death of him that dieth, saith the Lord God: wherefore turn your-selves, and live ye.

AARON: *(Breaks away from the scene, comes to one side of the stage as choir continues to sing quietly in the background.)* Things around the inn are different now. Grandfather says that the birth of the new King caused Father to have a change of heart. I guess he's right. Father took our finest silver cup to give to the new King that night, but he said it was a poor gift. He said that it couldn't compare to the gift the King gave to us. I never saw what gift Father got, but it must be wonderful because he's so happy all the time. It's funny, he's not so worried about attracting the richest guests any more. We don't have as much money as we used to either, but he laughs and smiles, and he doesn't scold like he used to do. And, he tells everyone who comes to stay at our inn the story about the baby, the King of Kings, Lord of Lords, Wonderful, Counselor, Almighty God, the Everlasting Father, the Prince of Peace who was born in our own stable, right here in Bethlehem.

COME FOLLOW ME (Choir)

SEEK HIM WITH HASTE
by
Carolyn Gifford

Reader 1 -- Female
Reader 2 -- Male
Reader 3 -- Female or Male
Plus **Choir (SATB) and soloists (optional)**

NOTE: This is a format or structure for the addition of appropriate Christmas songs, carols or hymns. You may use the songs suggested in the script or substitute some of your own choosing. But, REMEMBER, that ALL music should be purchased from the publishers and/or respective local music or bookstores and that no copies should be made of the songs. The mention of the songs in this script implies no inherent right to use that song without proper purchase of the music.
Original Music for the script:
Silent Night / Sing Out Silent Night SATB is available from the publisher, *www.shiningsharonmusic.com*, at no cost.

Reader 1: "And what does Christmas mean to you?"
Reader 2: A teacher asked a bright-eyed child.
Reader 3: "Oh--Christmas is surprises and secrets that we're not 'sposed to tell."
Reader 1: "Christmas means new toys and clothes--and

Grandma's fudge!"

Reader 2: another cried.

Reader 1: "I like the snowflakes,"

Reader 2: a young boy said,

Reader 1: "and cookies with frosting--and candy canes, too!"

Reader 3: "Christmas is magic,"

Reader 2: an older child added,

Reader 3: "cause people are nicer and want to do good."

Reader 2: A girl in the corner hesitated then stood.

Reader 1: "But these things aren't Christmas--not really,"

Reader 3: she said.

Reader 1: "Christmas means JESUS--that's the best part of all."

Reader 2: How simple a response and yet such a powerful truth. At this holiday season we experience the excitement and pleasures of surprises, gifts and homemade treats.

Reader 1: We DO feel a magic in the air as "hearts are opened to a new measure of kindness." But, as this young child expressed, "the best part of all" is the birth of the Holy Child we commemorate on this day----Jesus Christ, the Son of God----

Reader 3: the newborn King of Kings.

(Silent Night) (In the first performance we used a new arrangement of "Silent Night" with an original contrapuntal or descant called "Sing Out Silent Night")

Reader 2: Have you ever gazed up into the night sky at its myriad of stars and wondered about heaven--and life--and the eternities beyond? To our finite minds there is so much that we cannot fully understand or even begin to comprehend.

Reader 1: Christ said, "This is my work and my glory to bring to pass the immortality and eternal life of man." Yes, man WILL live forever, and this is because of the Lord's birth, death, and resurrection. It is a gift of love, freely given, from God on High. And though the magnitude of this miracle is far beyond our understanding, we've been given the Holy Spirit--to testify and bear witness within of the truthfulness of Christ's mission.

Reader 3: "For God so loved the world that he gave his only Begotten Son, that whosoever believeth in him should not perish but have everlasting life."

(I WONDER AS I WANDER -- SATB or another appropriate song)

Reader 2: In the book of Luke we read:

Reader 3: "The angel Gabriel was sent from God unto a city of Galilee, named Nazareth, to a virgin espoused to a man whose name was Joseph...and the virgin's name was Mary. And the angel came in unto her and said,

Reader 1: "Hail, thou that art highly favoured, the Lord is with thee: blessed art thou among women....And behold, thou shalt conceive in thy womb, and bring forth a son, and shalt call his name JESUS. He shall be great, and shall be called the Son of the Highest....

Reader 2: And Mary said, Behold the handmaid of the Lord; be it unto me according to thy word."

Reader 1: Many years before this sacred encounter, the prophet Nephi received his own vision of this most holy event.

Reader 2: He records: "And an angel...said unto me: Nephi, what beholdest thou? And I said: A virgin, most beautiful and fair above all other virgins. And he said unto me: Knowest thou the condescension of God? And I said: I know that he loveth his children...(Then) he said unto me: Behold, the virgin whom thou seest is the mother of the Son of God, after the manner of the flesh. And it came to pass that I beheld that she was carried away in the Spirit; and after she had been carried away in the Spirit for the space of a time the angel spake unto me, saying: Look! And I looked and beheld the virgin again, bearing a child in her arms. And the angel said unto me: Behold the Lamb of God, yea, even the Son of the Eternal Father!"

(AWAY IN A MANGER -- SATB)

Reader 3: A story is told of a young boy named who was asked to play the part of the Innkeeper in the Christmas Pageant that year. As it came time for him to sternly turn Mary and Joseph away, his own heartfelt emotions overcame him. "Begone!" the prompter whispered from backstage. "Begone!" the boy repeated automatically. But as he watched Joseph sadly lead Mary away, tears filled

Seek Him With Haste

his eyes as he called out, "Don't go, Joseph. Bring Mary back. You can have MY room."

Reader 1: Perhaps each one of us has felt that same way. Had we been the innkeeper, SURELY we would have recognized their great need and offered shelter to the stranger.

Reader 2: Today there are many who are seeking refuge and in need of warmth and protection.

Reader 3: There are those seeking solace from illness or disease.

Reader 1: Others are in need of every day comforts we often take for granted.

Reader 2: The world is filled with people who are "knocking at the door" seeking for a sense of belonging and yearning for something (or someone) to believe in. It doesn't take much to extend a word of kindness, a gift of friendship, or a message of hope. What sweet refuge we can offer with a listening ear, a caring heart, or a helping hand.

Reader 3: The Savior said, "For I was an hungered, and ye gave me meat: I was thirsty, and ye gave me drink: I was a stranger, and ye took me in: Naked, and ye clothed me: I was sick, and ye visited me: I was in prison, and ye came unto me.---Verily, verily, I say unto you, In as much as ye have done it unto the least of these my brethren, ye have done it unto me."

Reader 1: "Oh, may I have compassion for the stranger, Remembering that baby in a manger!
That night there was no room in the inn;

This night may there be room within--
Within my heart for him."

(ROOM IN THE INN -- SATB)

(SCRIPTURAL READING for **"ANTHEM of CHRIST"**
a beautiful Choral background that already has a narrative
set to it. This narrative might be able to be substituted
using the music to **"Anthem of Christ"** or another
appropriate song could be "hummed," "oohed," or
"ahhed" in the background)

(MUSIC begins. Then start this reading on the third beat of
measure nine of "**Anthem Of Christ**")

Reader 1: For unto us a child is born, unto us a son is
given: and his name shall be called Wonderful,
counsellor, the mighty God, the everlasting Father, the
Prince of Peace.

Reader 2: For behold, the time cometh, that with power,
the Lord Omnipotent who reigneth...shall come down
from heaven among the children of men, and shall dwell
in a tabernacle of clay, and shall go forth amongst men
working mighty miracles...and lo, he shall suffer
temptations, and pain of body...even more than man can
suffer...And he shall be called Jesus Christ, the Son of
God, the Father of heaven and earth, the Creator of all
things.

Reader 3: And there were in the same country shepherds

Seek Him With Haste

abiding in the field, keeping watch over their flock by
night. And lo, the angel of the Lord came upon them, and
the glory of the Lord shone round about them; and they
were sore afraid. And the angel said unto them, Fear not:
for, behold, I bring you good tidings of great joy, which
shall be to all people. For unto you is born this day in the
city of David, a Saviour, which is Christ the Lord.

Reader 1: And it came to pass that while (the Nephites)
were conversing one with another, they heard a voice as if
it came out of Heaven...and they cast their eyes up....and
saw a man descending, clothed in a white robe...and he
stretched forth his hand...saying, "Behold I am Jesus
Christ whom the prophets testified shall come into the
world. Behold I am the light and the life of the world."

Reader 2: When the Son of man shall come (again) in his
glory, and all the holy angels with him...he shall sit upon
the throne and (gather all nations)...and shall say unto
them on his right hand, Come ye blessed of my Father,
inherit the kingdom prepared for you.

Reader 3: What doth the Lord require of thee but to do
justly and to love mercy and to walk humbly with thy
God.

Reader 1: Behold, this is my work and my glory, to bring
to pass the immortality and eternal life of man.
        (MUSIC ends)

Reader 2: The shepherds were personally invited on that
holy night to undertake a search for the babe in a manger.
They said one to another,

Reader 3: "Let us go now unto Bethlehem--and they came with haste."

Reader 1: The wise men also sought out the Christ and found him. Those who are wise--still seek Him today.

Reader 2: The prophet Moroni said,

Reader 3: "I commend you to seek this Jesus whom the prophets and apostles have written."

Reader 1: No quest is so universal--no undertaking so richly rewarding. As we seek Christ and repledge ourselves to doing his work, we shall learn to forget ourselves and turn our thoughts to the greater benefit of others.

Reader 2: This is the spirit of Christ--the true spirit of Christmas--and it can be with us not just for one day each year, but as a companion always.

Reader 3: Jesus, himself, lovingly admonished, "Come Follow Me."

Reader 1: He whose birth we commemorate this season is more than the symbol of a holiday. He is the Son of God,

Reader 2: the Creator of the earth,

Reader 3: the Redeemer of Mankind,

All Three: the Prince of Peace.

(OH COME ALL YE FAITHFUL -- SATB with Congregation joining on fourth verse)

THE END

THAT IT MIGHT BE FULFILLED...

by Myrth Burr

CHARACTERS

Reader

Narrator

Children in Primary (maybe only selected classes)

NOTE: This is a format or structure for the addition of appropriate Christmas songs, carols or hymns. You may use the songs suggested in the script or substitute some of your own choosing. But, REMEMBER, that ALL music should be purchased from the publishers and/or respective local music or bookstores and that no copies should be made of the songs. The mention of the songs in this script implies no inherent right to use that song without proper purchase of the music.

Primary: SONG -- "Once Within A Lowly Stable"

Congregation: SONG -- "Oh, Little Town Of Bethlehem"

Reader: Luke 2:1-14 And it came to pass in those days, that there went out a decree from Cæsar Augustus, that all *the* world should be *taxed*.

2 (And this *taxing* was first made when Cyrenius was governor of Syria.)

3 And all went to be taxed, every one into his own city.

4 And Joseph also went up from Galilee, out of the city of Nazareth, into Judæa, unto the city of David, which is called *Bethlehem;* (because he was of the house and lineage of David:)

5 To be taxed with Mary his *es*poused wife, being great with child.

6 And so it was, that, while they were there, the days were accomplished that she should be delivered.

7 And she brought forth her *first*born son, and wrapped him in swaddling clothes, and laid him in a manger; because there was no room for them in the *inn.*

8 And there were in the same country shepherds abiding in the field, keeping watch over their flock by night.

9 And, lo, the angel of the Lord came upon them, and the *glory* of the Lord shone round about them: and they were sore afraid.

10 And the angel said unto them, Fear not: for, behold, I bring you *good* tidings of great *joy,* which shall be to all people.

11 For unto you is *a born* this day in the city of David a *Saviour,* which is Christ the *Lord.*

12 And this *shall be* a *sign* unto you; Ye shall find the babe wrapped in swaddling clothes, lying in a manger.

13 And suddenly there was with the angel a multitude of the heavenly host praising God, and saying,

14 *Glory* to God in the highest, and on earth *peace,* good

That It Might Be Fulfilled

will toward men.

Narrator: Jesus' birth in Bethlehem was heralded by
angels, advertised by the shepherds and celebrated by the
Kings from the east. But to the King in the land of His
birth He was taken as a threat. King Herod in his efforts
to eliminate this threat "Sent forth and slew all the
children in Bethlehem two years old and under." Joseph,
having been forewarned in a dream, arose in the night and
took the young child and His mother and departed into
Egypt to await the death of King Herod. Thus it might be
fulfilled which was spoken by the prophet saying, "Out of
Egypt have I called My Son. When King Herod had died,
Joseph was told that he should take Mary and Jesus and
return to Israel. Thus it was that they came to settle in
Nazareth that yet another prophecy might be fulfilled --
"He shall be called a Nazarene." Little is known of Jesus'
childhood and early manhood. Luke 2:40 gives a little
insight into his early life: "And the child grew and waxed
strong in spirit, filled with wisdom: and the grace of God
was upon Him."

**Primary: SONG -- "They Found Him Teaching In The
Temple"**

Reader: Luke 2: 46-51
46 And it came to pass, that after three days they found him
in the *temple,* sitting in the midst of the *doctors, both*
hearing them, and *asking* them questions.
47 And all that heard him were astonished at his

31

understanding and answers.

48 And when they saw him, they were amazed: and his mother said unto him, Son, why hast thou thus dealt with us? behold, thy father and I have sought thee sorrowing.

49 And he said unto them, How is it that ye sought me? *wist* ye not that I must be about my *Father's* business?

50 And they understood not the saying which he spake unto them.

51 And he went down with them, and came to Nazareth, and was *a subject* unto them: but his mother kept all these sayings in her heart.

Narrator: From the scripture it is supposed that Joseph was a carpenter and Jesus did learn the trade. From yet other scripture we may conclude that He had at least four brothers and some sisters. His development was as real and as necessary as that of all children. Over His mind had fallen a veil of forgetfulness common to all who are born to earth. "He received not of the fulness at first but received grace for grace. And Jesus increased in wisdom and stature, and in favor with God and man."

Reader: Matt 3: 1-3

In those days came John the Baptist, preaching in the wilderness of Judæa,

2 And saying, *Repent* ye: for the *kingdom* of heaven *is* at hand.

3 For this is he that was spoken of by the prophet *Esaias,* saying, The *voice* of one crying in the wilderness, *Prepare* ye the way of the Lord, make his *paths* straight.

That It Might Be Fulfilled

Primary: SONG -- (Your Choice)

Reader: Matt 3: 13-17

13 Then cometh Jesus from Galilee to Jordan unto John, to be *bap*tized of him.

14 But John forbad him, saying, I have need to be baptized of thee, and comest thou to me?

15 *A*nd Jesus answering said unto him, *Suffer it to be so* now: for thus it *becometh* us to *fulfil* all righteousness. Then he suffered him.

16 And Jesus, when he was *bap*tized, went up *straightway* out of the water: and, lo, the heavens were opened unto him, and he saw the *Spirit* of God descending like a *dove,* and lighting upon him:

17 And lo a *voice* from heaven, saying, This is my *beloved Son,* in whom I am well pleased.

Narrator: After Jesus was baptized He commenced His ministry in Galilee, first in the city of Nazareth and then in Capernaum that still the prophecy might be fulfilled. And Jesus began to preach and to say "REPENT: for the kingdom of Heaven is at hand.

Congregation: SONG -- "I Know That My Redeemer Lives"

Reader: Matt 19: 13-15

13 Then were there brought unto him little children, that he

should put *his hands* on them, and pray: and the disciples rebuked *them.*

14 But Jesus said, *Suffer* little *children,* and forbid them not, to come unto me: for of such is the kingdom of heaven.

15 And he laid *his* hands on them, and departed thence.

Primary: Class Five should move to a picture that illustrates the following scripture:

Reader: Matt 25: 34-40

34 Then shall the King say unto them on his *right* hand, Come, ye *blessed* of my Father, *inherit* the *kingdom* prepared for you from the foundation of the world:

35 For I was an *hungered,* and ye *gave* me meat: I was thirsty, and ye gave me drink: I was a *stranger,* and ye took me in:

36 Naked, and ye clothed me: I was sick, and ye *visited* me: I was in *prison,* and ye came unto me.

37 Then shall the righteous answer him, saying, Lord, when saw we thee an hungered, and fed *thee?* or thirsty, and gave *thee* drink?

38 When saw we thee a stranger, and took *thee* in? or naked, and clothed *thee?*

39 Or when saw we thee *sick,* or in prison, and came unto thee?

40 And the King shall answer and say unto them, Verily I say unto you, Inasmuch as ye have *done it* unto one of the *least* of these my *brethren,* ye have done *it* unto me.

That It Might Be Fulfilled

Congregation: SONG -- "I Heard The Bells On Christmas Day"

Speaker: (2-5 minute talk) <u>Subject:</u> I know that Christ lives today

Narrator: The wise men followed the star to Bethlehem to give Jesus gifts of gold, Frankincense and Myrrh to honor and recognize the birth of a King. We can also pay homage to our Savior, just as the Wise Men did, and we can do it all throughout the year.

Speaker: (2-5 minute talk) Blessings I have received from giving.

Speaker: The Bishop

Congregation: SONG -- Joy To The World.

THERE WILL BE PEACE
by Myrth Burr

READER 1
READER 2
CHOIR

NOTE: This is a format or structure for the addition of appropriate Christmas songs, carols or hymns. You may use the songs suggested in the script or substitute some of your own choosing. But, REMEMBER, that ALL music should be purchased from the publishers and/or respective local music or bookstores and that no copies should be made of the songs. The mention of the songs in this script implies no inherent right to use that song without proper purchase of the music.

Once the music begins there should be no break in the musical accompaniment. Narration should be delivered over intros and playouts.

Reader 1: The birth of Christ, the Anointed One, was foretold by the Prophet Isaiah in the Holy Land, also in the Promised land -- America. For ninety years, during the reign of the Nephite Judges, great signs and wonders were given unto the people as the words of the prophets began to be fulfilled. Angels appeared, and wise men declared unto the people tidings of great joy as signs and miracles were wrought among the people who believed in the words of the Prophet Samuel, the Lamanite.

There Will Be Peace

Reader 2: As the people began to rejoice in the prospects of His coming, the non-believers taunted them saying, "You foolish ones! Your joy and your faith concerning these things hath been in vain. Nothing is going to happen!" A great uproar began throughout the land with contentions and threats being made against the faithful believers. Some began to be very sorrowful. Their faith wavered -- lest by any chance or by the slightest means those things which were spoken might not come to pass. Never the less, they did watch steadfastly for that day and night and another day that should be as one period of light which would herald the advent of the Savior's mortal life.

Reader 1: A day was set apart by the unbelievers, in which all those who believed in those traditions should be put to death, except the sign, spoken by the beloved Samuel, should come to pass. When the new prophet, Nephi III, saw the wickedness of his people, his heart was exceedingly sorrowful. He went out and bowed himself down to the earth and cried mightily all the day to his God in behalf of his people. Those whom he loved were about to be slain because of their faith.

Reader 2: But in tenderness and compassion the Voice of the Lord came from the spirit world. Christ, the Ruler, appeared unto Nephi saying, "Lift up your head and be of good cheer; Behold, The time is at hand. On this night shall the sign be given. On the morrow come I into the world to show unto the world that I will fulfill all that which I have caused to be spoken by the mouths of my prophets. Behold, I come unto my own, to fulfill all things which I have made known unto the children of men from the foundations of the world."

Reader 1: So in ancient, quiet Bethlehem, the spirit world, and the mortal world awaited the Savior's birth. He, a promised Son of David.

SONG: "O, Little Town of Bethlehem" or "The Star Carol"

Reader 2: All Christendom reveres the words -- by angels sung and shepherds heard. Those who comforted Mary and assisted Joseph in the weeks that followed could not have known, without inspiration, What Child Is This that lay sleeping on a bed of hay. The angel chorus proclaimed it.

SONG: "What Child Is This?"

Reader 1: The glad news that touched the hearts of believers throughout the world, in the meridian of time, has radiated out through the ages, impelling our spirits toward righteousness and peace. Listen again -- understand.

SONG: "Hark, The Herald Angels Sing"

Reader 2: In the silence of the night, those who long for peace and love the Lord are filled with the conviction of the Lord's divine birth. The words, so simply spoken over

There Will Be Peace

one hundred years ago, have become a symbol of the spirit of the Christmas celebration.

SONG: "Silent Night"
MUSICAL PASSAGE: Instrumental solo

Reader 1: Through the ages of misery and suffering, when both heaven and earth have wept, Christians have longed for peace even when at war. The Holy night was observed briefly by weary warriors. During the Franco-Prussian War of the last century, all paused as righteous men, caught in a terrible turmoil, lifted their voices and renewed their hearts to the French carol "Cantique de Noel."

SONG: "O, Holy Night"

Reader 2: The story is told of a stalwart German Soldier who responded, in his native tongue, to enunciate the mutual hope for peace to be brought by the Savior.

SONG: "Von Himmel Hoch"

Reader 1: Now, at Christmas time, amid the dissolution of nations and war among people unaccustomed to the freedom to exercise their agency, we pause. hate is strong. It mocks the song of peace on earth, good will toward men. The world still longs for that peace promised by the angels. Joy can enter our hearts as we reflect, knowing that as we learn His word and follow His ways there will be peace in the hearts of men.

SONG: "I Heard The Bells On Christmas Day"

Reader 2: With Zion enlarging her borders, Saints can learn to rejoice. In the silence of the night, let us sleep in heavenly peace.

SONG: "Silent Night" Last verse

The End.

AMERICA'S FIRST CHRISTMAS
by Myrth Burr

CHARACTERS

NARRATOR

READER (is the voice of Samuel The Lamanite, the people of Nephi III, Jesus Christ; or they can be portrayed by three separate readers.)

CHOIR with optional soloists

NOTE: This was meant to provide a framework for a Christmas Sacrament meeting or Fireside, and the music should be selected to fit the available talents and tastes of those performing it. THREE copies required.

SONG: Your Choice (CONGREGATION)

Narrator: Samuel The Lamanite had cried repentance for many days in the great city of Zarahemla but the people had cast him out. He was about to return to his own city when the voice of the Lord came to him. It commanded him to go back and prophesy to the people whatsoever things should come into his heart. When he reached the gates of the city he was met by angry people. So, he ascended to the wall of the city and stretched forth his hands and cried with a loud voice to the people below:

Reader (As Samuel): "Behold, I give unto you a sign; for five years more cometh and then cometh the Son Of God to redeem all who shall believe upon His name. And this I give unto you for a sign of His coming: There shall be great lights in the heaven--insomuch that the night before He cometh there shall be no darkness and there shall be a day a night and a day as if it were a day. And behold, there shall a new star arise such as ye have never beheld and this also shall be a sign unto you. And another sign I give unto you. A sign of His death; for He must surely die that salvation may come to all. And on the day that He suffers death, the sun shall be darkened and refuse to give light. And also the moon and the stars, and there shall be no light for the space of three days, until He shall rise again from the dead. behold, I stand upon the walls of this city that you might know of the conditions of repentance and ye might receive a remission of your sins through Jesus Christ, the Son of God.

SONG: Come Follow Me (CHOIR)

Narrator: many people heard these words. Some believed and rejoiced, others hardened their hearts against them. The years slipped by. There were many wo said that the time was past for the words of Samuel to be fulfilled and they rejoiced over their brethren and mocked them, saying,

Reader (As people of Nephi III): Your joy and your faith have brought you nothing -- for the time is passed."

Narrator: And a day was set that all who believed should be put to death except the sign be given. Their leader, Nephi, felt a great concern for his people. It troubled him to see so many without faith that they should plot the death of those that were righteous. He went out and bowed himself down in humble prayer for his people. All day he cried unto the Lord. As the time for night drew near, a voice came to him saying:

Reader (As Jesus): Be of good cheer, for behold the time is at hand. On this night the sign shall be given and on the morrow come I into the world.

SONG: Your Choice (CHOIR with SOLOIST)

Narrator: And it came to pass as Jesus had said, for the sun went down, but there was no darkness. The people were astonished. Many of them fell to the earth for they began to know that the Son of God must surely appear. From east to west, from north to south -- over the whole land they began to fear; for had not the prophet testified of these things.

SONG: Your Choice (CHOIR)

Narrator: A new star appeared in the heavens and the hearts of the righteous rejoiced because it was as Samuel, the prophet, had decreed. Nephi went forth among the people, teaching them, and baptizing them in great numbers. Wickedness ceased for a season and peace came over the face of the whole land.

SONG: Your Choice (CHOIR with CONGREGATION)

Christmas Programs For Sacrament Meetings

LIFT UP YOUR HEAD
AND BE OF GOOD CHEER
by Carolyn Gifford

This program was designed originally to involve the Bishop's family. His wife and each of his children took turns narrating the words. It is easily adaptable to any family but we still recommend that the long section in the middle of the piece be spoken by the Bishop of the Ward.

There are 3 (THREE) original compositions that can go along with this piece:

> **O, Holy Child** by Carolyn Gifford and C. Michael Perry (a PDF of the SATB arrangement is available for $15.00 -- this includes the right to photocopy up to 25 copies of the song for your choir. Go to *www.shiningsharonmusic.com* or call us)

> **Samuel Tells of the Baby Jesus** is available in the Children's Songbook. However, there is a descant that was written for this version that is available for free from *www.shiningsharonmusic.com,* or call us.)

> **A New Star** by Carolyn Gifford and C. Michael Perry. (a PDF of the SATB arrangement is available for $15.00 -- this includes the right to photocopy up to 25 copies of the song for your choir. Go to *www.shiningsharonmusic.com* or call us)

Christmas Programs For Sacrament Meetings

CHOIR: "Good Christian Men Rejoice" found in Christian Hymn Books

MOTHER: At this joyous Christmas season, people from all ends of the earth unite in celebrating the birth of God's only begotten Son, Jesus Christ, the Savior of the world.

BISHOP: Prophets of the Old Testament foretold this blessed event and proclaimed the good news that the Messiah would be born. Book of Mormon prophets likewise bore witness of His coming and spoke of signs that would be given before the Christ-child's birth.

MOTHER: The prophet Alma taught: "For behold...there be many things to come; and...there is one thing which is of more importance than they all--for...the time is not far distant that the Redeemer liveth and cometh among his people...and behold, he shall be born of Mary...a precious and chosen vessel, who shall...conceive by the power of the Holy Ghost and bring forth a son, yea, even the Son of God.

CHOIR: "O Holy Child" *(Original Song) or choose another*

YOUNGEST SON: Samuel the Lamanite was another Book of Mormon prophet who testified of the Savior's birth. His mission was not an easy one. Samuel was commanded to preach repentance unto the Nephites who, at that time, were a predominantly wicked people and did not obey God's commandments.

Lift Up Your Head And Be Of Good Cheer

OLDEST SON: Despite Samuel's continued preachings and warnings of destruction, the Nephites hardened their hearts and refused to receive his message. Though the people cast him out, the Lord instructed Samuel to return and prophesy those things he would "put into his heart."

YOUNGEST SON: The Nephites refused to let Samuel enter their city, so he stood upon the outer wall, stretched forth his hands, and began prophesying unto them. The words Samuel spoke made the people angry and many of them threw stones and shot arrows at him. But God protected Samuel because he had an important heavenly message to share.

OLDEST SON: Samuel said unto them: "I give unto you a sign for five more years cometh, and behold then cometh the Son of God to redeem all those who shall believe on His name...Therefore, there shall be one day and a night and a day, as if it were one day and there were no night; and this shall be unto you for a sign; and it shall be the night before (the Son of God) is born."

CHILDREN'S CHOIR: "Samuel Tells of the Baby Jesus" *(with original CHOIR descant) or do without descant.*

YOUNGEST DAUGHTER: The Christmas story, as told in the New Testament, talks about angels proclaiming the message of Christ's birth to the shepherds. Likewise, it was an angel that appeared unto Samuel the Lamanite and commanded him to deliver this same sacred message to the Nephites. Is it any wonder that such a holy event was accompanied by heavenly messengers and other God-given signs?

BISHOP: Samuel prophesied, "Behold there shall a new star arise, such an one as ye never have beheld; and this also shall be a sign unto you, and it shall come to pass that ye shall be amazed, and wonder, insomuch that ye shall fall to the earth."

CHOIR: "A New Star" *(Original Song) or choose another.*

MOTHER: Though there were many Nephites who mocked Samuel and rejected his teachings, there were also many who did believe his words and desired to repent. These believers turned to Nephi, confessed their sins, and were baptized.

OLDEST DAUGHTER: Time passed and the signs and wonders spoken of by the prophets began to be fulfilled. Still there were disbelievers who said "it is not reasonable that such a being as a Christ shall come...Why will he not show himself in this land as well as in the land of Jerusalem?" And Satan did stir them up to do iniquity and to harden their hearts against that which was good and against that which should come.

MOTHER: The division amongst the Nephites became so great that a wicked plan was set up to have all the believers killed. Many people cried out, saying: "Behold the time is past and the words of Samuel are not fulfilled;

therefore your faith concerning this thing hath been vain."

OLDEST DAUGHTER: Imagine the sorrow and concern the people must've felt who believed in Samuel's message! Not only was their faith being mocked and ridiculed, but the lives of their children and other loved ones were now being endangered because of that faith. How tempting it would have been to deny the spiritual witness they had received in order to avoid the contention and now the impending threat of death itself from those around them.

MOTHER: But the people held onto their beliefs, and in spite of the fear they must've experienced, they united together in their sincere hope that Christ indeed would come into the world as the prophets had testified.

CHOIR (with optional vocal solo): "I Believe in Christ"

BISHOP: As Bishop, there have been many times when I have gone to the Lord in prayer seeking His counsel and guidance concerning the members of this ward. These have been sacred experiences where I've felt the Lord's love and have received answers and direction. Such experiences are personal and humbling, yet I know because of them that the Lord is aware of each one of us--He knows our feelings and concerns, and He answers our prayers.

I can't help but think of Nephi and the great sorrow he must've felt as he witnessed the persecution of his people--the people he served and taught and loved. With heaviness in his heart he turned to the Lord "and cried mightily...in behalf of his people, yea, those who were about to be destroyed because of their faith...And it came to pass that he cried mightily unto the Lord all that day."

(And this is the part that stands out in my mind): "...behold, the voice of the Lord came unto him, saying: "Lift up your head and be of good cheer; for behold, the time is at hand, and on this night shall the sign be given, and on the morrow come I into the world, to show unto the world that I will fulfill all that which I have caused to be spoken by the mouth of my holy prophets."

Imagine the joy and peace Nephi must've felt! "And...the words which came unto Nephi were fulfilled...for...at the going down of the sun there was no darkness and the people began to be astonished, and there were many who fell to the earth and began to fear because of their iniquity and their unbelief."

But for Nephi, and all those who had believed, this was a glorious time--for they knew that the Lord would be born because of the sign which had been given.

ORGAN SOLO: "O Holy Night"

MOTHER: How blessed we are to live at a time when modern-day prophets act as God's messengers to proclaim His holy word. Even amidst verbal stones and arrows, these divinely-appointed leaders continue to testify that Christ did come into the world, that he died for our sins, and that He still lives today.

OLDEST DAUGHTER: We, too, can be counted among the believers by having faith in the Lord and by following the direction of his chosen prophets. As we overcome the temptations of the world, we become like the new star-- pointing the way and guiding those who are searching to worship the Prince of Peace. Through Christlike actions we become a beacon, bearing witness of His goodness and encouraging others to believe on His name.

MOTHER: At this Christmas season, may we "lift up our head and be of good cheer" for the Son of God did indeed come to earth. May we rejoice in knowing that He shall come again, as the prophets have testified, and shall restore peace--a peace which surpasseth all understanding--in his kingdom here on earth.

CHOIR AND CONGREGATION: "Joy to the World"
THE END

www.ingramcontent.com/pod-product-compliance
Lightning Source LLC
Chambersburg PA
CBHW071737020426
42331CB00008B/2062